Seashore

Written and
photographed by

Colin S.Milkins

Artist: Sarah Beatty

Wayland

STARTING ECOLOGY

Pond and Stream

Seashore

Wasteland

Wood

Editor: Sarah Doughty

First published in 1993 by
Wayland (Publishers) Ltd
61, Western Road, Hove
East Sussex, BN3 1JD, England

British Library Cataloguing in Publication Data
Milkins, Colin S.
Seashore. - (Starting Ecology Series)
I. Title II. Series
574.909

ISBN 0 7502 0822 8

Typeset by Dorchester Typesetting Group, England
Printed in Belgium by Casterman S.A.

What is ecology?

Ecology is the study of the way plants and animals live together in a habitat. A scientist who studies this is called an ecologist. An ecologist finds out about a habitat by observing the area and carrying out experiments. If you do the projects in this book, you will be an ecologist too.

Always go to the seashore as a group with a parent or teacher, and never wander off on your own.

CONTENTS

The words in **bold** are explained
in the glossary on page 30.

The seashore

▲ *The seashore is the land covered and uncovered by the tide.*

The seashore lies between the land and the sea. This is an area where plants and animals live. Perhaps you have visited the seashore and noticed that sometimes the sea is close in and sometimes it is far away. The movements of the sea are called the tides.

Twice a day, there is a high tide and a low tide. Tides are caused by the pull of the sun and moon. A high tide is when the sea is closest to the land. A low tide is when the sea is farthest away.

There are many animals that live on the seashore. They **adapt** to the water coming in and out.

◄ *A harbour with the tide out.*

On a rocky shore, rocks and rock pools are good places for animals to live when the tide is out. Some animals, like mussels and barnacles, close their shells tightly and only open them to feed when the tide comes in.

On sandy shores, many animals, like cockles, live burrowed beneath the surface. They only come out to feed when the tide comes in and covers them over.

Try and visit the seashore nearest to where you live. The beach may be rocky, sandy or pebbly, but you will find a wide variety of sea life if you look carefully.

▶ *This is the same harbour with the tide in. Look at the yellow boat in both pictures.*

Seawater

▲ *The water that runs to the sea from rivers may pick up salts from the rocks.*

When rain falls on land it soaks into the ground or flows directly into ponds, streams and rivers. If the water drains through earth and rocks it will pick up **minerals** and become slightly salty, before it joins a river and flows into the sea.

Find out how salty seawater and fresh water are. Collect a small amount of seawater in a dish. Collect the same amount of fresh water from a pond in another dish. Put both dishes on a warm radiator or leave by a sunny window for a few days. The heat will make the water **evaporate** leaving the salt behind.

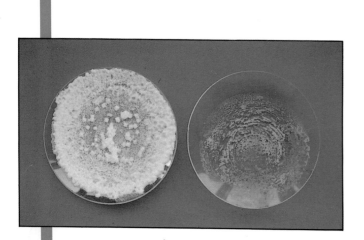

◄ *Is the dish that held seawater on the left or right?*

Which dish has the most salt in it? Why was it important to use the same amount of water in each dish for this experiment?

Find out how well things float in seawater and in fresh water. First make a 'floater' with a straw and a piece of plasticine, like the one in the diagram on the right. Make markings on the straw at 5 mm intervals.

Put your floater in a jar of pond water. Count how many marks there are above the water surface. Now do the same with seawater. Does the plasticine float higher in seawater?

Make a list of the plants and animals that live only in the sea and those that live only in ponds.

A floater in water. Find out if it floats higher in seawater or pond water.

Necklace-shell snail

On a sandy shore, most animals live under the surface. This man is digging for worms to use as bait.

Most of the animals that you find on a sandy shore live buried in the sand. Among these are many different types of cockles. Cockles have two halves to their shells. When the shell is closed, the cockle is safe from most **predators** on the seashore, except the necklace-shell snail.

The necklace-shell snail can eat the cockle even when the shell is closed. The snail uses its rasping tongue to bore a hole through the cockle's shell. The soft parts of the cockle can then be eaten.

When the cockles have been eaten or have died, you can find their shells on the shore. Some of them are very beautiful.

Make a collection of 100 shells from the seashore. Look at each shell very carefully. Any that have neat round holes in them were killed by the necklace-shell snail.

Put the shells with holes in one group. Put the other shells in another group. Count the number of shells in each set. Now draw a bar graph of your results like the one in the diagram on this page. One bar shows the number of cockles killed by the necklace-shell snail. The other bar shows the number of cockles that died in other ways.

Did the necklace-shell snail kill most of the cockles in your collection?

▶ *The necklace-shell snail has a coiled shell. Look for holes in the shells of the cockles.*

Number of cockles that died in other ways

Number of cockles killed by the necklace-shell snail

▲ *Draw a bar graph to show how many cockles were killed by the necklace-shell snail, and how many died in other ways.*

Barnacles

▲ *Seaweeds sweep over these rocks when the tide is in.*

▲ *Can you see the barnacles growing on this groyne?*

Young barnacles are sea creatures that begin their lives as **larvae** drifting among **plankton** in seawater. By the time they are ready to settle down on a rock, they look a little like small beans. The larvae fix themselves to a hard surface, and slowly grow into adult barnacles.

Adult barnacles have hard shells which they close tightly. They attach themselves firmly to rocks.

You will not find many barnacles on shores that have a lot of seaweed. This is because the seaweed swirls around in the **current** when the tide is in. The current sweeps the barnacle larvae off the rock before they can get a grip.

Barnacles feed when the tide comes in and covers them over. It can be fun watching barnacles feed. Find a small stone with a few barnacles on it. Place this stone in a plastic tumbler. Add some clear seawater and watch very closely.

▲ *The four smallest bean shapes in this picture are the barnacle larvae.*

The barnacle's shell will slowly open. Then a **tentacle**, which looks like a hand, will come out of the shell and start combing the water. Any small pieces of food in the water will be caught by the 'hand'. This food will then be eaten by the barnacle.

When you have finished watching the barnacle, put the stone back where you found it.

▶ *A barnacle combing the water for food.*

Limpets

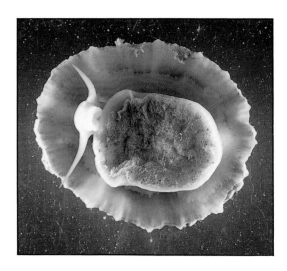

▲ *The underside of a limpet.*

Limpets are a kind of snail. They can attach themselves very tightly to rocks. To get a limpet off the rock you need to give it a sharp but gentle sideways knock. It will then fall off. If it does not come off with the first tap, it will be impossible to get off. This is because the limpet has a powerful 'foot' that squeezes the shell down hard on to the rock whenever it feels in danger.

Put your limpet upside-down in a tumbler of seawater. Look at its gills, tentacles, foot and eyes. When you have finished looking at it, put the limpet back carefully where you found it. This is its home.

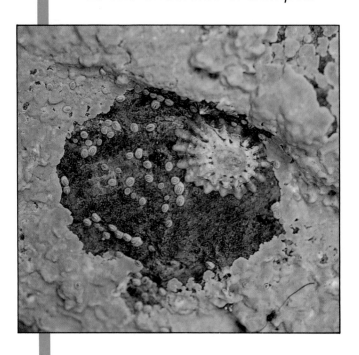

◄ *A limpet in a rock pool.*

If you are able to return to the beach the next day, you can see if your limpet has moved far from its home.

Put a little blob of white paint on the limpet's shell. Put another blob on the rock next to the limpet.

When the tide comes in the limpet will leave its home and search for food. When the tide has gone back out, you should return to where you found your limpet the day before. Now look for the white blob on the rock and search for your limpet.

Did your limpet come back to the place on the rock where you put the white blob?

► *Marks made by a limpet's rasping tongue.*

Groynes

Groynes are long walls or barriers that stop the sea from washing the beach away. They are a good place to look for sea creatures when the tide is out. You will find lots of animals that live on groynes such as limpets and barnacles. You may also find other things – such as fishermen's nets – hung up on them.

▲ *Pools at the ends of groynes contain lots of interesting sea creatures.*

▼ *These children are looking for shrimps in the groyne pool.*

Look at the seaweeds growing on the groyne. You will probably find green or brown seaweeds. Some brown seaweeds have little bubbles at the end of the leaves which help the seaweed to float when the tide comes in. Is the type of seaweed you find the same at the top and bottom end of the groyne?

When the tide goes out, there is sometimes a pool of water left at the furthest end of the groyne. Pull a net through the top layer of sand in the pool. You might be lucky and catch a shrimp in your net. Shrimps live in the sand and only come out to feed when the tide comes in, or when it is dark. Shrimps are well-**camouflaged** against the sand so you will have to look very carefully.

If you find a shrimp, make a little pool in the sand. Put the shrimp in your pool. What does the shrimp do?

▶ *Can you see the camouflaged shrimp?*

> **Warning:** The water in the pool can be quite deep.

▲ *Nowadays, fishermen's nets are made of nylon, which never rots away.*

Mussels

◄ These mussels are in a gap in the groyne.

Mussels can be found on rocks and groynes. Their shells may be covered in barnacles. Find a clump of mussels, and slowly pull one away. You will notice it is held on to the others by strings. Keep pulling and it will come away, without hurting the mussel.

Put the mussel in a tumbler of seawater. How long does it take for the shell to open?

Watch the mussel carefully. You will notice that two holes appear. These holes are called siphons. One of the siphons has frilly edges. The other has smooth edges.

The mussel sucks water in through one of the siphons. Tiny pieces of food in the water are taken in and eaten by the mussel. When the food has been removed, the water is pumped out through the other siphon.

Find out which siphon sucks water in. To do this, mix a small amount of baker's yeast with a little drop of seawater. Drop a little of the mixture near the siphons. See which siphon is drawing the yeast in.

When you have finished looking at your mussel, put it back on the rock or groyne where you found it.

▶ *These mussels are feeding. Look at their siphons. Each mussel has one siphon with a frilly edge and another with a smooth edge.*

▲ *Feeding a mussel with baker's yeast.*

Dogwhelks

▲ *Dogwhelks sitting on mussels. The dogwhelks are boring holes through the mussels' shells.*

Look for dogwhelks on groynes and rocks. They are sea creatures that have a strong, snail-like shell. If you look for dogwhelks in the spring you may find them with their **egg capsules**.

Dogwhelks are predators that feed on **prey** such as mussels and barnacles. They eat mussels by boring a hole through the mussel's shell. It takes about three days to bore the hole. So, if you find a dogwhelk sitting on a mussel, it will be boring a hole. Pull the dogwhelk off and you will see the partly-made hole. You will have saved the mussel's life too.

◄ *Dogwhelks and their egg capsules.*

With your friends, try to count all of the mussels on the groyne. You will have to **estimate** the number of mussels that are in large clumps, and then count the number of large clumps you find. Sort your data into sets of ten. Now count the number of dogwhelks on the groyne. Sort this data into sets of ten, too.

Show your data as a pyramid like the one in the diagram below. What does the diagram tell you about the number of predators and prey?

▲ *A striped dogwhelk shell and some mussel shells. Can you see the hole in each mussel's shell?*

▼ *A pyramid showing numbers of prey and predators.*

Set of 10 dogwhelks   Set of 10 mussels

Rock pools

▲ *A rock pool.*

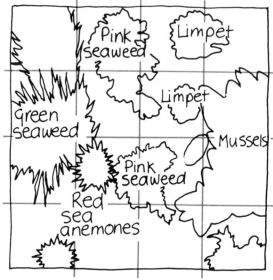

▲ *Plan of the rock pool.*

When the tide goes out, seawater can be left behind in rock hollows. These rock pools are like miniature seas. They contain lots of animals and plants that need to be in water all of the time.

Look carefully into a rock pool. Pool **gogglers** will help you to see beneath the surface. Lots of the animals are hiding from you under the rock ledges. See what happens when you drop some minced meat into the pool. Small fish, crabs and prawns will come out to eat the meat.

Which of these animals gets to the food first? How long does it take for the animals to sense that there is food about?

Make a note of all the animals and plants you see in the rock pool. You may find sea anemones attached to the rocks, waving their tentacles for food. You may see tube worms – creatures which build tubes of mud, sand or bits of shell in which they live. Crabs and starfish crawl over underwater rocks, and if you are lucky you may see a fish called a blenny.

Draw a **plan view** of the rock pool you have seen, like the one in the diagram on the opposite page. Label the plants and animals you have found.

▲ *This is a hermit crab. Hermit crabs make homes inside snail shells. They can be found in rock pools.*

▼ *These children are looking in a rock pool using rock pool gogglers to help them.*

Warning: Be careful near a rock pool as the rocks can be slippery and the pool may be deep.

Slipper limpets

▲ *A pile of four slipper limpets. Can you see each one?*

In some rock pools you should find slipper limpets. They form a pile, one on top of the other. The slipper limpets at the bottom of the pile are the biggest and oldest. These are the females. The slipper limpets at the top of the pile are the smallest and the youngest. These are the males. The strange thing is, that as the males grow older they change into females. They will end up at the bottom of the pile as females.

Find a pile of slipper limpets. Use **callipers** to measure the length of the largest female at the bottom of the pile. Now measure the length of the smallest male at the top of the pile.

Draw a line showing the length of the female on a piece of card. Draw another line showing the length of the male.

Now collect as many empty slipper limpet shells as you can find. Compare each one with the lines that you have drawn on the card to see if the animal was male or female.

How many shells in your collection were males when they died? How many were females when they died?

Look at the shape of the shells. Why do you think they are called slipper limpets?

▶ Lay each of your empty shells near the lines you have drawn. Decide whether each slipper limpet was male or female when it died.

▲ Some empty slipper limpet shells. Why do you think they are called slipper limpets?

Length of female slipper limpet from pile

Length of male slipper limpet from pile

Sea anemones

You should find some sea anemones in your rock pool. When they are closed they look just like little blobs of red or green jelly. When they are open, look at the tentacles with your pool gogglers. These tentacles contain many thousands of special stinging cells. They are used to catch and **paralyse** prey.

A fish being swallowed by a sea anemone. It only takes a minute for this to happen.

Don't be afraid to touch the tentacles yourself. They will feel sticky, but your skin is too thick to be stung. If the anemone has folded away its tentacles, feed the anemone with minced meat. Its tentacles will soon unfold.

▲ *A sea anemone. The tentacles and the blue blobs contain thousands of stinging cells.*

Carry out a feeding experiment on your anemone. Try dropping tiny pieces of the following foods on to the tentacles:

▼ *A plumose sea anemone. These are only found in very deep water.*

1. Chocolate
2. Bread
3. Cheese
4. Crisps
5. Minced meat

Which of these foods does the anemone catch with its tentacles and eat?

Which of these foods does it reject? Do other anemones do the same?

The strand line

▲ *Lots of interesting things can be found on the strand line. What can you see in this picture?*

There are lots of objects floating in the sea. When the tide starts to go out some of these are left on the shore. They form a line called the strand line. It is interesting to go searching for things along the strand line.

Sometimes dead animals get washed up. You may find the body of a dead crab, or a sea bird covered in oil. Oil gets into the sea when it is accidentally spilt. Sometimes the captains of oil tankers break the law by cleaning out their tanks with seawater. This is very dangerous for sea life.

◄ *A cuttlefish 'bone' or shell. This was once inside the cuttlefish's body.*

You will find all kinds of shells on the beach. If you are lucky you may find the white shell of the cuttlefish. Unlike lots of sea creatures that have shells on the outside, the shell of the cuttlefish is like a bone and is inside its body.

Another common find on the strand line is what looks like dead seaweed. This is not a plant at all. It is the remains of a **colony** of tiny animals called Flustra. Look at the surface closely. Each little hole that you see once had a tiny animal in it.

▲ *The remains of dead crabs.*

▼ *This is called Flustra. It is the remains of a colony of sea creatures.*

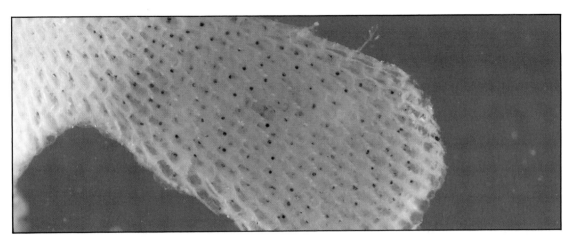

27

A nature trail

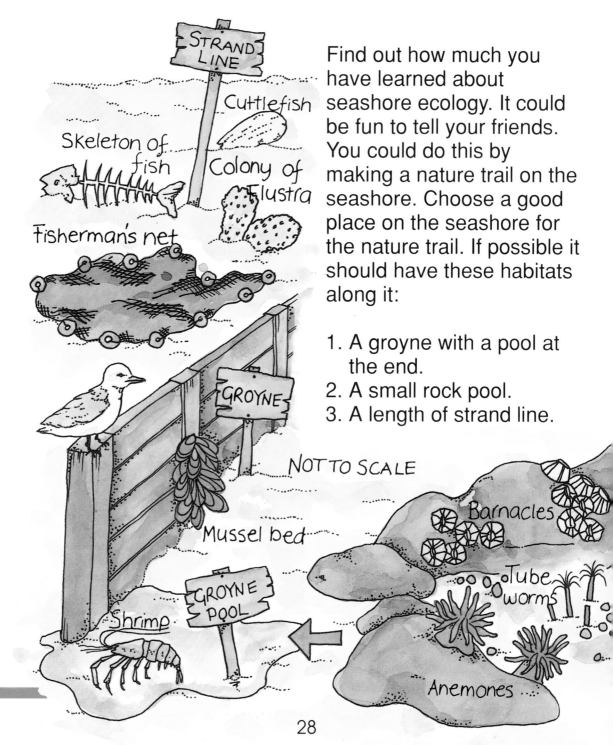

Find out how much you have learned about seashore ecology. It could be fun to tell your friends. You could do this by making a nature trail on the seashore. Choose a good place on the seashore for the nature trail. If possible it should have these habitats along it:

1. A groyne with a pool at the end.
2. A small rock pool.
3. A length of strand line.

28

Look carefully at your nature trail. How do you want people to walk around it? Draw some arrows on cards. Put them on sticks to show the way.

Make some habitat name cards – and put these in the right places on your nature trail.

Now make some information cards. These can be taken around the trail by your friends. Write on them the following:

1. The name of the habitat.
2. What someone might look for in the habitat. For example, limpet, barnacle or cuttlefish shell.
3. Some more information of your own.

A seashore nature trail.

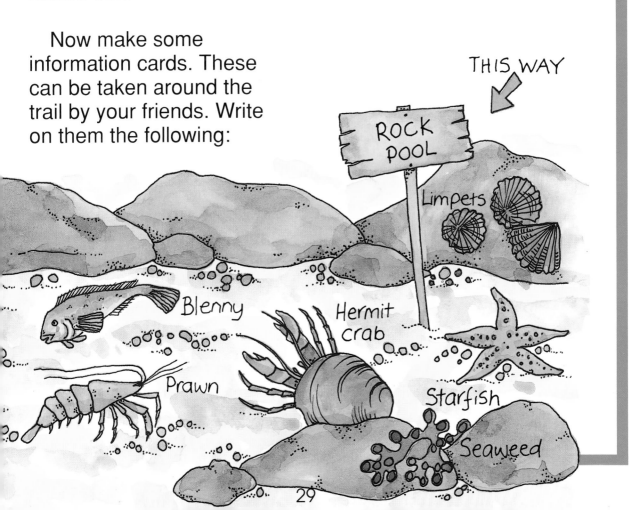

GLOSSARY

Adapt To change or adjust.
Callipers Hand-held instruments with two steel legs that can help to measure things.
Camouflaged When something is coloured to match its background.
Colony Lots of animals of the same type living together.
Current The flow of water in a sea or river.
Egg capsules Little containers in which eggs are laid.
Estimate To roughly work out the quantity of something.
Evaporate To dry up. Water turns into vapour in the sun or warmth.
Gogglers A hollow tube that is used to look in rock pools. Clear plastic over one end is held in place with an elastic band.
Larvae The young of certain animals.
Minerals Non-living substances that form in rocks.
Paralyse To become unable to feel or move.
Plankton Very small animals and plants that drift in water currents.
Plan view To look at something from overhead.
Predators Animals that kill and eat other animals.
Prey Animals that are killed and eaten by other animals.
Tentacle The thin, easily-bent, arm-like part of certain animals.

BOOKS TO READ

Bellamy, D. **The Rock Pool** (Macdonald, 1988)
Jennings, T. **Sea and Seashore** (OUP, 1981)
Parker, S. **Seashore** (Dorling Kindersley, 1989)
Vaughan J. **By the Seashore** (Macdonald, 1989)
Watts, B. **Rock Pools** (A & C Black, 1985)

NOTES

This book involves learning about ecology through practical activities at the seashore and is a suitable reference for use in the classroom. It is recommended that the activities for children should only be carried out under the supervision of a teacher.

p6-7 This investigation will enable children to understand that seawater and fresh water may look alike but are different physically because of the large amount of salt dissolved in seawater. Encourage children to think about what would happen if marine plants and animals were placed in fresh water or if fresh water animals and plants tried to survive in the sea.

p8-9 The shells to be collected are not those of the true cockle. They are more likely to be shells of similar molluscs such as tellins, banded wedge shells and trough shells. The term cockle is used for convenience. It is important that the children collect the first hundred shells they find, and not to look specially for shells with holes in them. Usually the resulting bar graph shows that more cockles died from other causes than being killed by necklace-shell snail.

p10-11 Often a barnacle-encrusted mussel will suffice as a 'stone'.

p14-15 There are usually three types of seaweed to be found on the shore - red, green or brown. The green seaweeds are found mostly below the high tide mark. Brown seaweeds often cover much of the shore. Red seaweeds usually grow at the low tide mark. Shrimps usually only come to the surface when the tide comes in, or it is dark. Your shrimp will probably try to hide in the sand.

p16-17 The container the mussel is in must be kept perfectly still. The yeast particles will be sucked into the mussel through the frilly-edged inhalant siphon. Filter feeders such as mussels and barnacles become food for other animals. In this way the microscopic food particles are passed down the food chain, although they have not been eaten directly by the larger animals.

p20-21 There are lots of animals hiding in rock pools that are rarely seen by the casual observer. Using fresh minced meat, get the children to observe the way the animals feed. Try comparing animals that you find in a rock pool at the top of the shore with animals that you find in the middle shore. The lower shore is too dangerous for young children, unless they are in very small groups with at least two teachers present.

p22-3 Slipper limpets are found along the east coast, along the coast of the English Channel and around Wales. It may take a while to search for them. The statistical results of the experiment will vary, but the younger males would be expected to feature more prominently in the sample than the older females.

p24-5 In this investigation, usually only the foods that contain protein would be eaten by the sea anemone. However some anemones may like to eat other foods.

p26-7 Get the children to plan their nature trail before they go to the shore, bearing in mind that the people using the nature trail should be able to look at as much sealife as possible, but must cause no damage as they walk around. If you cannot go to the beach, you could make your nature trail as a classroom wall display instead.

INDEX